Scott Foresman
Reading

Grade 1
Phonics Reader 15

Ducks Have Fun!
by Kathy Mormile
illustrated by
Susan Edison

Phonics Skills:
• Short *u*
• Initial *s* blends

Scott Foresman
Phonics System

Scott Foresman

Ducks Have Fun!

by Kathy Mormile
illustrated by Susan Edison

This book belongs to

_____

Phonics for Families: This book features words with short *u*, as in *ducks* and s*u*n; words that begin with the letter *s* plus another consonant, as in *swim* and *small*; and the high-frequency words *more, time, sleep,* and *jump*. Read the book together. Then ask your child to go back through the story and say the words with short *u*.

Phonics Skills: Short *u*; Initial *s* blends

High-Frequency Words: *more, time, sleep, jump*

Scott Foresman

Reading

Grade 1

Phonics
Take-Home
Readers

Scott Foresman
Phonics System

Scott Foresman

Editorial Offices: Glenview, Illinois • New York, New York

Sales Offices: Reading, Massachusetts • Duluth, Georgia • Glenview, Illinois
Carrollton, Texas • Menlo Park, California

Editorial Offices
Glenview, Illinois • New York, New York

Sales Offices
Reading, Massachusetts • Duluth, Georgia • Glenview, Illinois
Carrollton, Texas • Menlo Park, California

ISBN 0-673-61258-9

6 7 8 9 10-CRK-06 05 04 03 02 01

TABLE OF CONTENTS

Phonics Readers for Unit 5

Book 25 **The Neat Green Cast**
Long e spelled *ea*; Inflected ending *-ed* (with and without spelling change: doubling final consonant)

Book 26 **Who Rang the Bell?**
Long a spelled *ai, ay*; Contractions

Book 27 **Duck Gets a New Coat**
Long o spelled *oa, ow*; Inflected ending *-ing* (with and without spelling change: doubling final consonant)

Book 28 **Dad's Gift**
Long i spelled *igh, ie*; Possessives (singular)

Book 29 **My Mail**
Vowel sounds of *y* (long e, long i); Compound words

Book 30 **Sue Blew a Big Bubble**
Vowel patterns *ew, ue*; Inflected ending *-es*; Plural *-es*

Phonics Readers for Unit 6

Book 31 **Stars**
R-controlled *ar*; Suffix *-ly*

Book 32 **Fox and Stork**
R-controlled *or*; Inflected endings *-s, -es, -ed, -ing* (with and without spelling change: drop e before adding *-ed, -ing*)

Book 33 **Cowgirl Gert and the Dust Storm**
R-controlled *er, ir, ur*; Comparative endings *-er, -est*

Book 34 **Funny Clowns**
Vowel diphthong *ow /ou/*; Medial consonants (two-syllable words)

Book 35 **How Hound Became Happy**
Vowel diphthong *ou /ou/*; Medial consonants (two-syllable words)

Book 36 **Roy Goes Camping**
Vowel diphthongs *oi, oy*; Multisyllabic words (compounds, contractions, inflected endings)

Now this duck wants to sleep.

It finds a good spot.

This duck had fun!

8

Ducks Have Fun!

by Kathy Mormile
illustrated by Susan Edison

Scott Foresman

Editorial Offices: Glenview, Illinois • New York, New York
Sales Offices: Reading, Massachusetts • Duluth, Georgia
Glenview, Illinois • Carrollton, Texas • Menlo Park, California

The sun is up.
It is time to have fun!

It got one bug.
But this duck wants more!

This duck looks for a snack.

It looks for bugs in the mud.

Ducks have fun in the water.

They like to swim.

Some ducks jump in the water.
This duck is going in!

4

Ducks like to eat too.

Some ducks eat small fish.

Some ducks eat bugs.

5

Grade 1
Phonics Reader 16

The Tub
by Kana Riley
illustrated by
Sharon Holm

Phonics Skills:
• Short *u*
• Initial *c*/s/ and *g*/j/

Scott Foresman

The Tub

by Kana Riley
illustrated by Sharon Holm

This book belongs to

_____

Phonics for Families: This book features words with short *u*, as in *bug* and *tub*, as well as the word *giraffe*, in which the letter *g* represents the /j/ sound, and the word *cement*, in which the letter *c* represents the /s/ sound. It also gives your child practice reading the high-frequency words *carry*, *bring*, *our*, *hold*, and *us*. After reading the book with your child, talk about working together and sharing.

Phonics Skills: Short *u*; Initial *c*/s/ and *g*/j/

High-Frequency Words: *carry, bring, our, hold, us*

But they all stop.

Look! The tub is big.
It can hold us all!

8

The Tub

by Kana Riley
illustrated by Sharon Holm

Scott Foresman

Editorial Offices: Glenview, Illinois • New York, New York
Sales Offices: Reading, Massachusetts • Duluth, Georgia
Glenview, Illinois • Carrollton, Texas • Menlo Park, California

Bugs dig in the mud.

Ducks jump in the tub.

The water is ours.
So it is our tub!

Giraffes jump in the tub.

Giraffes carry cement.

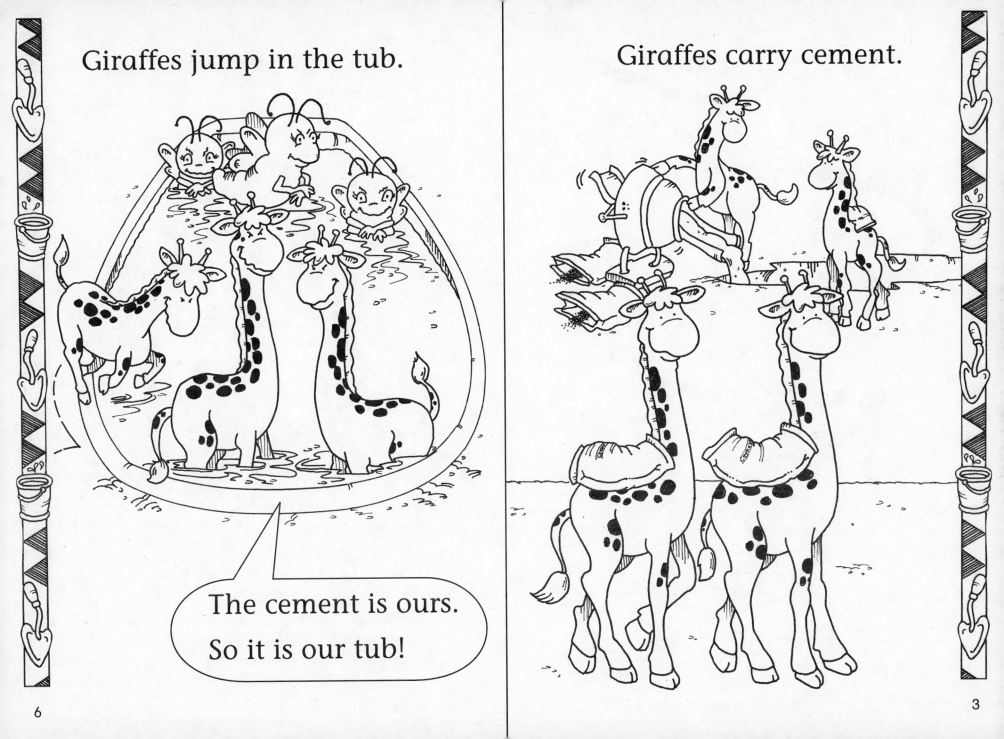

The cement is ours.
So it is our tub!

Ducks bring water.

Bugs jump in the tub.

We dug the mud.
So it is our tub!

4

5

Ken came out to play.

He wants to play ball.

He asks them all!

Yes, they all want to play!

8

Hop, Run, and Jump!

by B. G. Hennessy
illustrated by Valeria Petrone

Scott Foresman

Editorial Offices: Glenview, Illinois • New York, New York
Sales Offices: Reading, Massachusetts • Duluth, Georgia
Glenview, Illinois • Carrollton, Texas • Menlo Park, California

Pat came out to play.

She knows how to hop.

2

Will you jump with me?

The bug did not!

7

Jill came out to play.
She knows how to jump.

Will you hop with me?

The frog did not!

Tom came out to play.

He knows how to run fast.

Will you run with me?

The dog did not!

© Scott Foresman 1

Scott Foresman
Reading

Grade 1
Phonics Reader 18

Dogs Can't Read
by Robin Bloksberg
illustrated by
Michael Sloan

Phonics Skills:
- Short vowel pattern CVC
- Contractions

Scott Foresman
Phonics System

Scott Foresman

Dogs Can't Read

by Robin Bloksberg
illustrated by Michael Sloan

This book belongs to

_____

Phonics for Families: This book reviews short vowels and features contractions. It also provides practice reading the high-frequency words *say, please, read, word,* and *again*. Read the book together. Then have your child go back through the story and find words with short vowels, such as *not* and *sits*.

Phonics Skills: Short vowel pattern CVC; Contractions

High-Frequency Words: *again, please, read, say, word*

Can you read? No!
Dogs can't read.

Dogs Can't Read

by Robin Bloksberg
illustrated by Michael Sloan

Scott Foresman

Editorial Offices: Glenview, Illinois • New York, New York
Sales Offices: Reading, Massachusetts • Duluth, Georgia
Glenview, Illinois • Carrollton, Texas • Menlo Park, California

Ben has a little dog.

The dog can run and hop.

But the dog can't read.

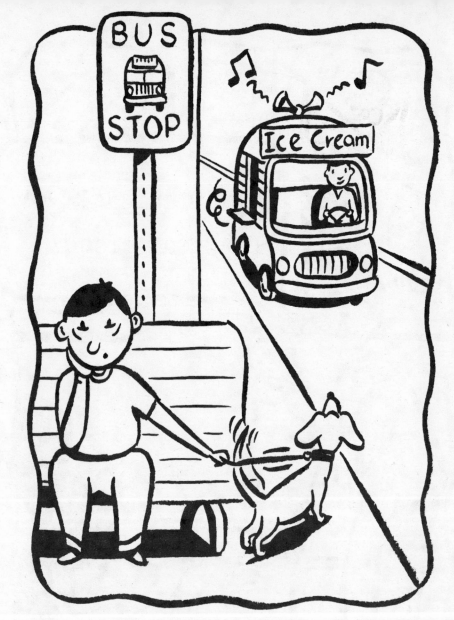

Ben sits down to rest.

What does the dog see?

Ben doesn't pick the flowers.
But his dog does!
The dog can't read.

They go for a walk.
Too bad the dog can't read!
The dog can't read a word.

Please don't get mad!
He's just a dog.
Dogs can't read.

Scott Foresman
Reading

Grade 1
Phonics Reader 19

The Missing Snake
by Maryann Dobeck
illustrated by
Lisa Blackshear

Phonics Skills:
• Long a (CVCe)
• Inflected ending –ed
  (without spelling change)

Scott Foresman
Phonics System

Scott Foresman

The Missing Snake

by Maryann Dobeck
illustrated by Lisa Blackshear

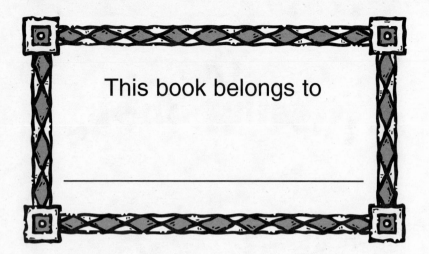

This book belongs to

_____

Phonics for Families: This book features words with long *a*, as in *snake* and *Jane*, as well as words ending with the letters *-ed*, as in *looked* and *yelled*. It also provides practice reading the high-frequency words *call*, *after*, *laugh*, and *something*. Read the book together. Then have your child name words that rhyme with *snake*.

Phonics Skills: Long *a* (CVCe); Inflected ending *-ed* (without spelling change)

High-Frequency Words: *call*, *after*, *laugh*, *something*

Dave laughed. He said,
"You are good. You cracked
the case!"

The Missing Snake

by Maryann Dobeck
illustrated by Lisa Blackshear

Scott Foresman

Editorial Offices: Glenview, Illinois • New York, New York
Sales Offices: Reading, Massachusetts • Duluth, Georgia
Glenview, Illinois • Carrollton, Texas • Menlo Park, California

My name is Jane.
Is something missing? Call
me. I can take the case.

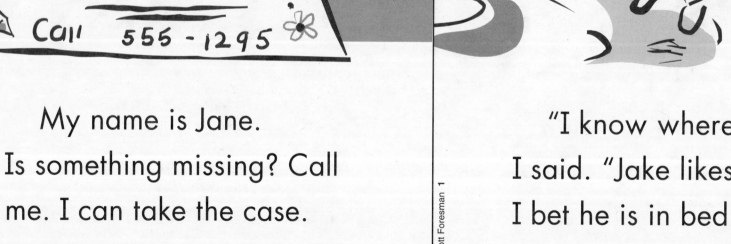

"I know where Jake is!"
I said. "Jake likes to sleep.
I bet he is in bed!"

"It is late," said Dave.
"It is time for bed."
"That's it!" I yelled.

I find missing planes.
I find missing canes. I
find missing skates.

Dave came to see me.

"Jake is missing," said Dave.

"Jake is my pet snake."

We looked some more.
We looked by the vase. We
looked by the gate.

We looked and looked.
We looked by the bed. We
looked by the games.

Dave looked for Jake.
He looked in his cage. He
looked in the tub.

8

5

Dave called Jake. He yelled
his name.

"You make me laugh," I said.
"A snake can not call back."

"Come with me," I said.
"I will go after Jake. I will
find him for you."

Scott Foresman Reading

Grade 1
Phonics Reader 20

Take the Cake
by Nat Gabriel
illustrated by
Remy Sinard

Phonics Skills:
• Long a (CVCe)
• Initial digraphs *ch, th*

Scott Foresman Phonics System

Scott Foresman

Take the Cake

by Nat Gabriel
illustrated by Remy Sinard

This book belongs to

_____

Phonics for Families: This book features words with long *a*, as in *cake*, and words that begin with the letters *ch* and *th*, as in *chop* and *then*. It also provides practice reading the high-frequency words *was*, *every*, *of*, *mother*, and *made*. Read the book together. Then go back through the story and have your child point out all the words with long *a*.

Phonics Skills: Long *a* (CVCe); Initial digraphs *ch*, *th*
High-Frequency Words: *was*, *every*, *of*, *mother*, *made*

Mother made the cake.

Blaze ran to save the cake.

Jane was there to take the cake.

And she will eat it too!

Take the Cake

by Nat Gabriel
illustrated by Remy Sinard

Scott Foresman

Editorial Offices: Glenview, Illinois • New York, New York
Sales Offices: Reading, Massachusetts • Duluth, Georgia
Glenview, Illinois • Carrollton, Texas • Menlo Park, California

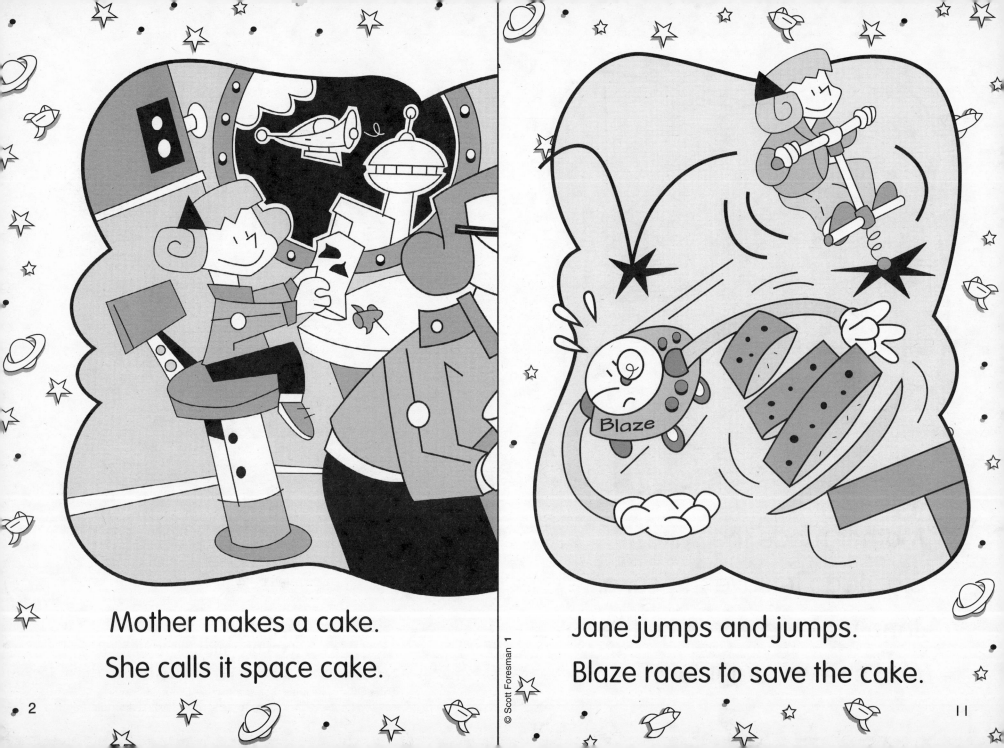

Mother makes a cake.

She calls it space cake.

Jane jumps and jumps.

Blaze races to save the cake.

© Scott Foresman 1

Mother has to fix the cake.

Then it looks good.

Blaze helps.

Blaze does the mixing.

A space cake has chips.

Blaze gets the cake.

He places it on a plate.

4

9

The cake is hot.

Mother and Jane play a game.

They play a game of chess.

Chop, chop, chop!

Chop, chop, chop!

A space cake has dates.

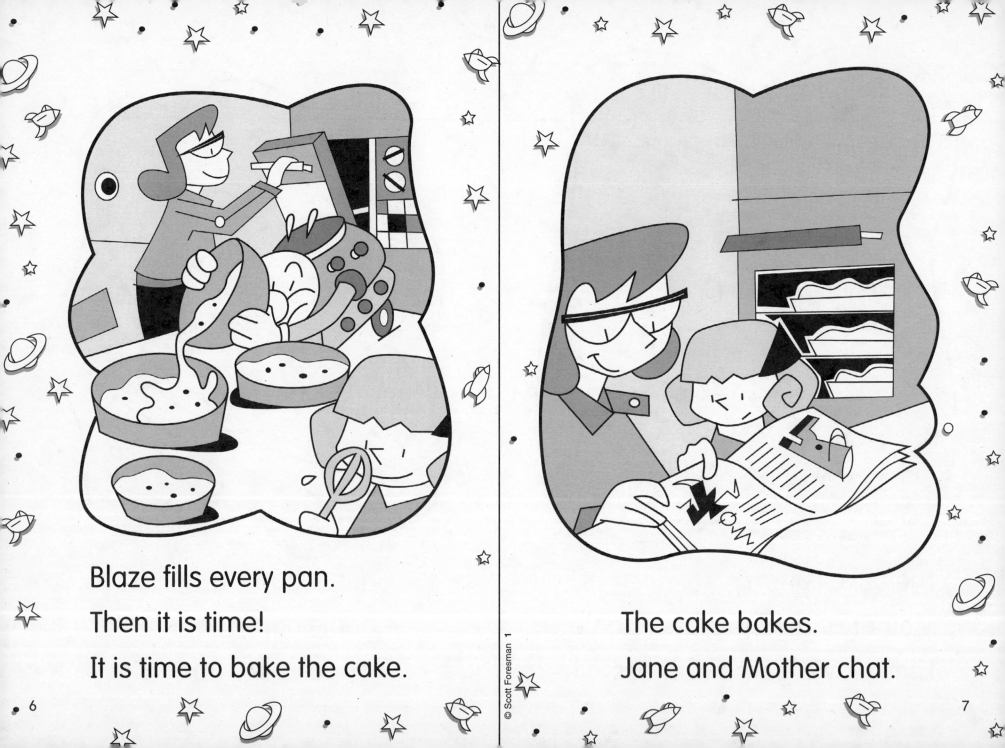

Blaze fills every pan.

Then it is time!

It is time to bake the cake.

The cake bakes.

Jane and Mother chat.

Scott Foresman
Reading

Grade 1
Phonics Reader 21

Whales
by Caitlin Tessier
illustrated by
Jon Weiman

Phonics Skills:
• Long *o* (CVCe)
• Initial digraph *sh*, *wh*

Scott Foresman
Phonics System

Scott Foresman

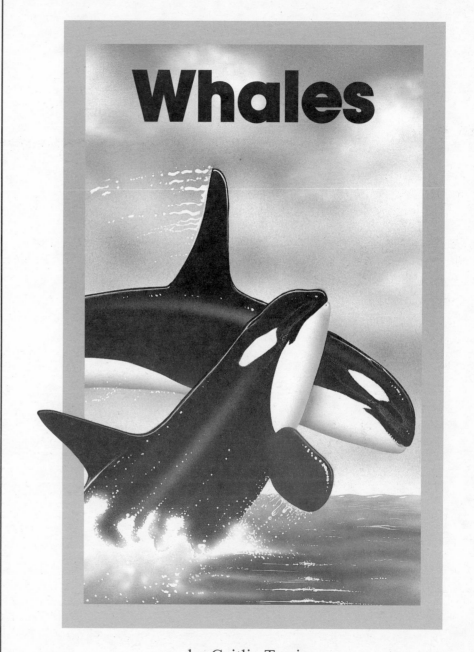

Whales

by Caitlin Tessier
illustrated by Jon Weiman

This book belongs to

_____

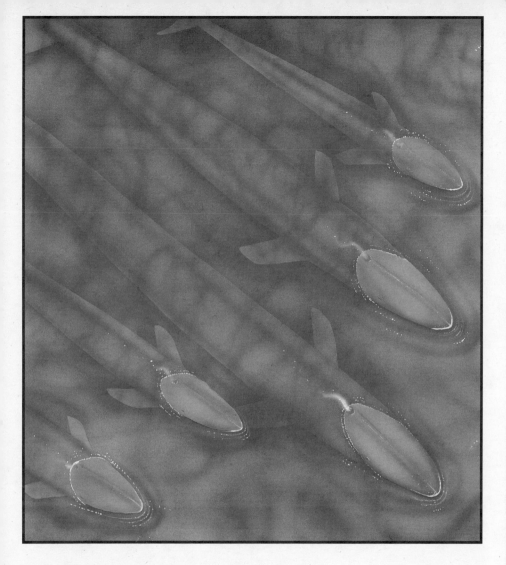

Whales swim here.

Whales swim there.

Whales are at home in the water.

Whales

by Caitlin Tessier
illustrated by Jon Weiman

Scott Foresman

Editorial Offices: Glenview, Illinois • New York, New York
Sales Offices: Reading, Massachusetts • Duluth, Georgia
Glenview, Illinois • Carrollton, Texas • Menlo Park, California

Whales swim in the water.

Whales swim and swim.

Whales are at home in the water.

Whales can do tricks.

This whale did a good job.

It gets a fish to eat.

It eats the whole fish!

Whales like to play.

They jump out of the water.

Father whales sing.

This ship looks for whales.

What do you see by the ship?

Is it a whale going by?

This is a blue whale.

Blue whales are very big.

This whale is as big as a bus.

© Scott Foresman 1

This whale has two holes.

The two holes are on the top.

In the water, the holes close.

This whale has a hole.

The hole is on the top.

In the water, the hole shuts.

This whale is little.

The little whale jumps.

It jumps out of the water!

Not all whales have teeth.

This whale does.

This whale does not.

Scott Foresman
Reading

Grade 1
Phonics Reader 22

Summer at Pine Lake
by Judy Nayer
illustrated by
Amy Young

Phonics Skills:
• Long *i* (CVCe)
• Medial consonants
  (single and double)

Scott Foresman
Phonics System

Scott Foresman

Summer at Pine Lake

by Judy Nayer
illustrated by Amy Young

This book belongs to

_____

Phonics for Families: This book gives your child practice in reading words with long *i,* as in *pine* and *like,* words with two-syllables, such as *pretty* and *muffins,* and the high-frequency words *be, friend, pretty, soon,* and *your.* Read the book with your child. Then have your child read aloud the words he or she finds with the long *i* sound.

Phonics Skill: Long *i* (CVCe); Medial consonants (single and double)

High-Frequency Words: *be, friend, pretty, soon, your*

Dear Diary,

It is time to go. But I'll be back again.

Your friend,

Mike

12

Summer at Pine Lake

by Judy Nayer
illustrated by Amy Young

Scott Foresman

Editorial Offices: Glenview, Illinois • New York, New York
Sales Offices: Reading, Massachusetts • Duluth, Georgia
Glenview, Illinois • Carrollton, Texas • Menlo Park, California

Dear Diary,

Soon it will be summer. The sun will shine. I will ride my bike. I will be out all the time.

Your friend,
Mike

2

Dear Diary,

We made muffins. We ate them with jelly. Yum!

Your friend,
Mike

11

Dear Diary,

    We went on a hike again. We went up a big hill. It was quite nice up there. I saw a pretty bird.

              Your friend,
              Mike

Dear Diary,

    Summer is here! The pretty flowers are out. Soon we will be at Pine Lake.

              Your friend,
              Mike

Dear Diary,

   We are at Pine Lake! It is very pretty here. I like our cabin.

   Your friend,

   Mike

© Scott Foresman 1

Dear Diary,

   We went to the lake again. Miles said, "Dive in!" So I did. The water was nice!

   Your friend,

   Mike

Dear Diary,

We got a pile of rocks.
We made a fire. We ate my
fish for dinner!

Your friend,

Mike

Dear Diary,

My friend Miles is here too.
He smiles all the time. His cat
had seven kittens! I like the
pretty little one.

Your friend,

Mike

Dear Diary,

We went on a big hike.
We walked a mile! I saw
five little rabbits. I got nine
pine cones.

Your friend,
Mike

6

Dear Diary,

We went to the lake. It was
very nice. I got a fish!

Your friend,
Mike

7

Scott Foresman
Reading

Grade 1
Phonics Reader 23

The Dude Ranch Dudes
by Amy Moses
illustrated by
Sharon Vargo

Phonics Skills:
• Long *u* (CVCe)
• Final digraphs *ch, tch, sh, th, ng;* Final nk

Scott Foresman
Phonics System

Scott Foresman

The Dude Ranch Dudes

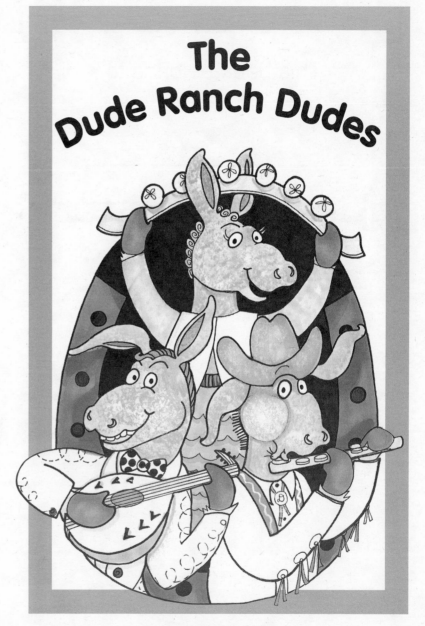

by Amy Moses
illustrated by Sharon Vargo

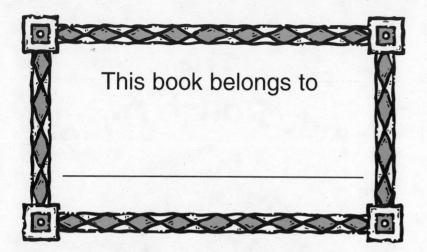

This book belongs to

_____

Phonics for Families: This book provides practice reading words with long *u*, as in *mule*; words that end with the letters *ch, tch, sh, th, ng,* and *nk*; and the high-frequency words *funny, were, four,* and *long*. Read the book together. Then have your child find all the words that have long *u* as in *mule*.

Phonics Skills: Long *u* (CVCe); Final digraphs *ch, tch, sh, th, ng, nk*

High-Frequency Words: *funny, were, four, long*

Soon the mules were doing it.

They did what Luke was doing.

It was so much fun!

The
Dude Ranch Dudes

by Amy Moses
illustrated by Sharon Vargo

Scott Foresman

Editorial Offices: Glenview, Illinois • New York, New York
Sales Offices: Reading, Massachusetts • Duluth, Georgia
Glenview, Illinois • Carrollton, Texas • Menlo Park, California

Luke woke up with pink spots.

He had four on his neck.

There were some on his legs.

There were some on his back.

© Scott Foresman 1

The mules stopped to watch.

They watched for a long time.

What was Luke doing?

The Dude Ranch Dudes sang.

Luke had to rub an itch.

He had to rub and rub!

"I itch," said Luke.

"So rub the itch," said Duke.

"I itch," said Luke.

"Don't rub it," said June.

"I think you have a rash."

Luke, June, and Duke left.

They went to the Dude Ranch.

4

9

"How will I sing?" Luke said.

"I wish I didn't itch."

But Luke did rub the itch.

Soon he had more spots.

"You look funny," said Duke.

"This rash is not funny,"
said Luke.

"How will I play?" Luke said.

"All I can do is rub my itch."

Scott Foresman
Reading

Grade 1
Phonics Reader 24

A Pack of Seeds
by B. G. Hennessy
illustrated by
Jane Chambless Wright

Phonics Skills:
• Long e spelled *ee, e*
• Compound words

Scott Foresman
Phonics System

Scott Foresman

A Pack of Seeds

by B. G. Hennessy
illustrated by Jane Chambless Wright

This book belongs to

_____

Phonics for Families: This book provides practice reading words with long *e*, spelled *ee* and *e*, as in *seeds* and *me*; compound words, such as *backpack*; and the high-frequency words *ask, kind, over,* and *any*. Read the book together. Then ask your child to find all the story words with long *e* spelled *ee* and *e*.

Phonics Skills: Long *e* spelled *ee, e*; Compound words
High-Frequency Words: *ask, kind, over, any*

Now I have lots of apples!

There are apples everywhere!

A Pack of Seeds

by B. G. Hennessy

illustrated by Jane Chambless Wright

Scott Foresman

Editorial Offices: Glenview, Illinois • New York, New York
Sales Offices: Reading, Massachusetts • Duluth, Georgia
Glenview, Illinois • Carrollton, Texas • Menlo Park, California

I saw a man.

He was walking over a hill.

The man looked funny.

I saw a man.

He was walking over a hill.

The man looked funny.

I wanted to keep the seeds.

The man said to plant them.

He had a pot on his head.

He had a backpack.

He was eating an apple.

I know that man.

He walks by himself.

He walks everywhere.

The man gave me some seeds.

He was very kind.

I looked inside the pack.

I saw seeds.

I ran to meet the man.

I wanted to ask him something.

Scott Foresman Reading

Grade 1
Phonics Reader 25

The Neat Green Cast
by Dona R. McDuff
illustrated by
Clive Scruton

Phonics Skills:
• Long *e* spelled *ea*
• Inflected ending -*ed*
  (with and without
  spelling change: double
  the final consonants)

Scott Foresman Phonics System

Scott Foresman

The Neat Green Cast

by Dona R. McDuff
illustrated by Clive Scruton

This book belongs to

_____

Phonics for Families: This book gives practice in reading words with the long *e*, spelled *ea*, as in *neat;* action words that end with the letters *ed,* as in *tipped* and *wanted;* and the high-frequency words *think, or, right, only,* and *buy.* Read the story together. Then ask your child to find all the words in the story that have long *e* spelled *ea.*

Phonics Skills: Long *e* spelled *ea;* Inflected ending *-ed* (with and without spelling change: double the final consonants)

High-Frequency Words: *think, or, right, only, buy*

Dean was at the shop.

I sat down next to him.

"What a neat cast!" he said.

"Want to go for a sled ride?"

I laughed. "Only in our dreams!"

12

The
Neat Green Cast

by Dona R. McDuff

illustrated by Clive Scruton

Scott Foresman

Editorial Offices: Glenview, Illinois • New York, New York
Sales Offices: Reading, Massachusetts • Duluth, Georgia
Glenview, Illinois • Carrollton, Texas • Menlo Park, California

Dean and I are friends.
One time we rode our sleds.
I wanted to beat Dean.
He wanted to beat me.

2

© Scott Foresman 1

"You look so sad," said Dad.
We'll go buy a treat."
We stopped for ice cream.

11

"Four weeks!" I said.
"That's too long!
What will I do?"

We were going fast.
I tipped over.
My sled tipped over too.
"Help me!" I yelled.
"I think I broke my leg!"

I went to the doctor.
She looked at me.
She checked my right leg.

"Your leg needs to heal.
This cast will help.
I'll check it in four weeks."

"Well," said the doctor.
"Do you want a green cast?
Or do you like blue?"
"Green is neat," I said.
"I want a green cast."

8

"Look," said the doctor.
"You broke your leg here.
Now we have to help it heal."

5

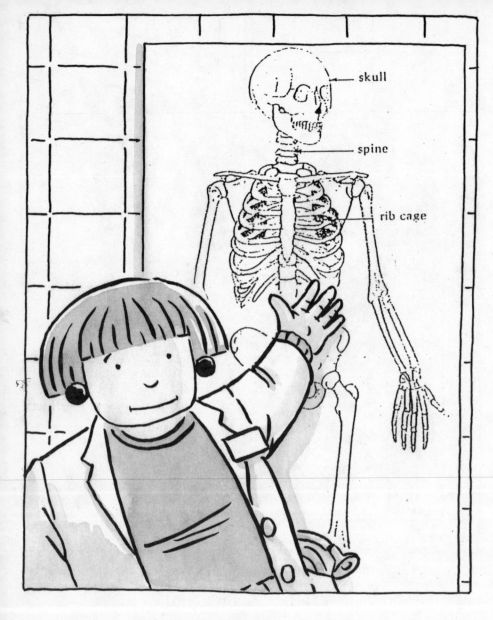

"You have 206 bones.
You broke only one of them."

6

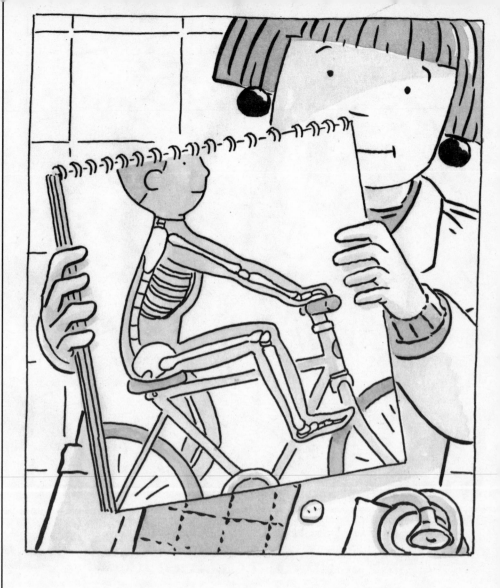

"Bones don't bend," she said.
"They help you run and play.
Bones are like a frame."

7

Scott Foresman
Reading

Grade 1
Phonics Reader 26

Who Rang the Bell?
by Sydnie Meltzer
Kleinhenz
illustrated by
George Ulrich

Phonics Skills:
• Long *a* spelled *ai, ay*
• Contractions

Scott Foresman
Phonics System

Scott Foresman

Who Rang the Bell?

by Sydnie Meltzer Kleinhenz
illustrated by George Ulrich

This book belongs to

_____

Phonics for Families: This book features words with the *ai* and *ay* spellings for long *a* and contractions such as *there's* and *it's*. It also provides practice reading the high-frequency words *when, from, live, don't,* and *hear.* Read the book with your child. Than have your child say words that rhyme with *Ray.*

Phonics Skills: Long *a* spelled *ai, ay;* Contractions
High-Frequency Words: *live, hear, don't, from, when*

"Wait!" yells Faith.
"Ray went up when we went out.
He made the bell ring!"

Who Rang the Bell?

by Sydnie Meltzer Kleinhenz
illustrated by George Ulrich

Scott Foresman

Editorial Offices: Glenview, Illinois • New York, New York
Sales Offices: Reading, Massachusetts • Duluth, Georgia
Glenview, Illinois • Carrollton, Texas • Menlo Park, California

Ray is our pet.

He does not stay in the tank.

He may walk all over.

Ding Ding Ding

The kids feed the birds.

They need more seeds.

Faith gets them from the desk.

Faith hears the fire bell!

"Who rang the bell?" the kids ask.

"We have been out all day," says Mary.

"No one was inside," says Vail.

"What is going on?" they ask.

The kids go out to paint.

Vail makes a mess.

He'll go in to clean up.

Boys

Vail can hear the fire bell!
It may mean there's a fire.
Vail runs out.

4

Mr. Bails runs outside.
"There is no fire," he says.
"Who rang the bell?" asks Jay.
"I don't know!" says Mr. Bails.

9

The kids go out the next day.
Jay needs a pail for sand.
Mrs. Fay lets Jay get it.
Jay hears the fire bell!

Mr. Bails runs out.
"There is no fire," he says.
"Who rang the bell?" asks Mrs. Fay.
"I don't know," says Mr. Bails.

"Who rang the bell?" the kids ask.
"We have been out all day," says May.
"What is going on?" they ask.

6

The kids go in.
Ray sits on a desk.
He wants to get some sun.

7

Scott Foresman
Reading

Grade 1
Phonics Reader 27

**Duck Gets
a New Coat**
by Judy Nayer
illustrated by
Laura Rader

Phonics Skills:
• Long *o* spelled *oa, ow*
• Inflected ending *-ing*
(with and without
spelling change:
doubling final
consonants)

Scott Foresman
**Phonics
System**

Scott Foresman

Duck Gets a New Coat

by Judy Nayer
illustrated by Laura Rader

This book belongs to

_____

Phonics for Families: This book provides practice in reading words with long *o* spelled *oa* and *ow*, as in *coat* and *show*; words ending with *-ing*, as in *looking* and *digging*; and the high-frequency words *new, old, her, show,* and *around*. After you read the book together, have your child first find the words with long *o* spelled *oa*, and then the words with long *o* spelled *ow*.

Phonics Skills: Long *o* spelled *oa, ow*; Inflected ending *-ing* (with and without spelling change: doubling final consonants)

High-Frequency Words: *new, old, her, show, around*

Duck ran all the way home.

She didn't think of stopping.

There it was.

Her new coat was in the box!

12

Duck Gets a New Coat

by Judy Nayer

illustrated by Laura Rader

Scott Foresman

Editorial Offices: Glenview, Illinois • New York, New York
Sales Offices: Reading, Massachusetts • Duluth, Georgia
Glenview, Illinois • Carrollton, Texas • Menlo Park, California

Duck had grown.
Her old coat didn't fit.
Duck needed a new coat.
She went shopping.

At last she asked Fox.
He was putting on socks.
Fox said, "I don't know.
Did you look in the box?"

She asked her friend Skunk.

She was loading her trunk.

She asked her friend Mole.

He was digging a hole.

Duck spent all day looking.

At last she saw a coat.

It fit her just right.

Duck got a new coat.

She was feeling good.

Duck went home.

She got her old coat.

Duck did not need it.

She gave it away.

She asked her friend Toad.

He was fixing the road.

She asked her friend Sheep.

She was towing her jeep.

She asked her friend Goat.

He was rowing a boat.

She asked her friend Crow.

She was paying for a show.

"I know what to do.

I'll go out," said Duck.

"I'll show everyone my new coat."

Duck looked all around.
She didn't see her coat!
"Help!" Duck moaned.
"My new coat is missing!"

Duck went all around.
She asked her friends.
"Did you see my new coat?"

Grade 1
Phonics Reader 28

Dad's Gift
by Judy Veramendi
illustrated by
Jackie Urbanovic

Phonics Skills:
• Long *i* spelled *igh, ie*
• Possessives (singular)

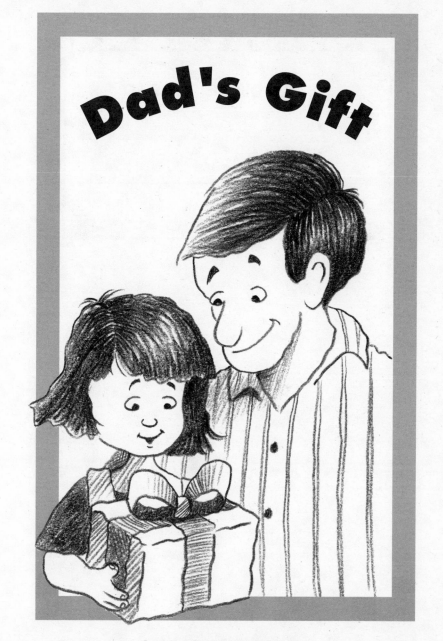

Dad's Gift

by Judy Veramendi
illustrated by Jackie Urbanovic

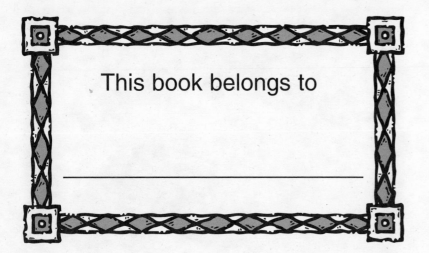

This book belongs to

_____

Phonics for Families: This book gives your child practice reading words with long *i* spelled *igh* and *ie*, as in *night* and *tied*; words that indicate possession, such as *Pam's;* and the high-frequency words *together, found, start,* and *first.* Read the book together. Then have your child find the story words that have long *i,* spelled *igh.*

Phonics Skills: Long *i* spelled *igh, ie*; Possessives (singular)

High-Frequency Words: *first, found, start, together*

It was a cat!

She picked up her dad's gift.

She held the cat tight.

It was just right!

Dad's Gift

by Judy Veramendi
illustrated by Jackie Urbanovic

Scott Foresman

Editorial Offices: Glenview, Illinois • New York, New York
Sales Offices: Reading, Massachusetts • Duluth, Georgia
Glenview, Illinois • Carrollton, Texas • Menlo Park, California

Pam had a pal.
Her pal's name was Jill.
They had fun together.

First Pam looked to her left.
She did not see anything.
Her dad said, "Look to the right!"
Pam saw something black.

Pam sighed.
Pam's mom said, "Come on!
Start looking!"

Jill had a little cat.
Jill's cat had a long tail.
The cat ran after its tail.

The cat was so cute.
It was very little.
It was just right for Jill.

Pam went to a bright light.
She read the note.

It was Pam's old stuffed cat.
A note was tied on its neck.
"This is not funny," said Pam.
"Read the note," said her dad.

Pam sighed.
"I want a cat like Jill's.
I'll play with it.
I'll play every night!"

One night Pam found a gift.
It was from her dad.

Pam asked, "What can it be?"
Her dad said, "Take a look!"

Scott Foresman
Reading

Grade 1
Phonics Reader 29

My Mail
by Kathy Mormile
illustrated by
George Ulrich

Phonics Skills:
• Vowel sounds of *y*
  (long *e*, long *i*)
• Compound words

Scott Foresman
Phonics System

Scott Foresman

My Mail

by Kathy Mormile
illustrated by George Ulrich

This book belongs to

_____

Phonics for Families: This book provides practice reading words with long *e* spelled *y*; words with long *i* spelled *y*; compound words; and the high-frequency words *their*, *most*, and *heard*. Read the book together. Then have your child find all the story words that have long *e* and long *i* spelled *y*. You might also show your child a piece of mail that was delivered to your home. Point out the address, return address, and the canceled stamp.

Phonics Skills: Vowel sounds of *y* (long *e*, long *i*); Compound words

High-Frequency Words: *their, most, heard*

Sally was right. It didn't take
long. I heard from my friends.
They got their mail. They were
very happy!

My Mail

by Kathy Mormile
illustrated by George Ulrich

Scott Foresman

Editorial Offices: Glenview, Illinois • New York, New York
Sales Offices: Reading, Massachusetts • Duluth, Georgia
Glenview, Illinois • Carrollton, Texas • Menlo Park, California

I like to get mail. Each day I check the mailbox. Most of the time, I don't get any. But it is fun to check anyway!

2

Sally tells me all about the mail. "When will my friends get their notes?" I ask.

"Soon!" Sally tells me.

I wave good-by as Sally drives away.

I walk over to Sally. I tell her
about my notes. I look in her truck.
There is so much mail!

I like to send mail too.
I send notes to my friends.
Each note needs a stamp.
Without a stamp, the note
will come back to me.

Today I am sending notes to my friends Kathy and Patty. They live in a big city.

Sally places the bin into the truck. Mom and I watch as she places a new bin inside the mailbox.

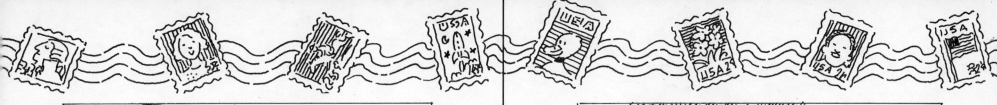

Sally gets out of the truck. She looks in the mailbox. Then she takes out a bin filled with mail.

I take my notes to the mailbox. It is only around the block. My mom walks with me. I drop my mail into the box.

We read the note on the mailbox. There is only one more pickup today. I think I will wait to see where my notes will go next!

6

Mom and I tell funny jokes as we wait. Soon a mail truck stops right by the mailbox.

7

Scott Foresman
Reading

Grade 1
Phonics Reader 30

**Sue Blew a Big
Bubble**
by Myka-Lynne Sokoloff
illustrated by
Andy Levine

Phonics Skills:
• Vowel patterns *ew, ue*
• Inflected ending *-es*
• Plural *-es*

Scott Foresman
Phonics System

Scott Foresman

Sue Blew a
Big Bubble

by Myka-Lynne Sokoloff
illustrated by Andy Levine

This book belongs to

_____

Phonics for Families: This book provides practice reading words with the vowel patterns *ew* and *ue,* as in *chew* and *clue;* action words that end with *-es;* plurals that are formed by adding *-es;* and the high-frequency words *better, people,* and *give.* Read the story together. Then ask your child to find the story words with the vowel patterns *ew* and *ue.*

Phonics Skills: Vowel patterns *ew, ue;* Inflected ending *-es;* Plurals *-es*

High-Frequency Words: *better, people, give*

Look at Sue!
She looks much better!
And she can blow a bubble too.

12

Sue Blew a Big Bubble

by Myka-Lynne Sokoloff
illustrated by Andy Levine

Scott Foresman

Editorial Offices: Glenview, Illinois • New York, New York
Sales Offices: Reading, Massachusetts • Duluth, Georgia
Glenview, Illinois • Carrollton, Texas • Menlo Park, California

This is Sue.
What's new with Sue?
Sue can blow a bubble.
She is big!

2

© Scott Foresman 1

First Mom kisses Sue.
Then she helps.
Sue gets a trim.

Sue finds her mother.
Mom knows what to do.

Here is little Sue.
Little Sue makes wishes.
What does she wish to do?
Here's a clue:

Sue can't see herself.
So she gets a few boxes.
Then she watches herself.
She chews and blows.
But she can't do it!

Pop!
The gum sticks like glue!
What does Sue do?
Here's a clue:

Sue doesn't know what to do.
She reaches for Drew.
He does not know what to do.

Sue watches people chew.
Most of all she watches Drew.
Drew teaches Sue.

Sue chews and chews.
Then Sue blows.
She blows till she is blue!
Sue doesn't give up.

One day, Sue blows and blows.
She blows a bubble.
It grows and grows and grows!

Scott Foresman
Reading

Grade 1
Phonics Reader 31

Stars
by Maggie Bridger
illustrated by
Tom Barrett

Phonics Skills:
• *R*-controlled *ar*
• Suffix *–ly*

Scott Foresman
Phonics System

Scott Foresman

Stars

by Maggie Bridger
illustrated by Tom Barrett

This book belongs to

_____

Phonics for Families: This book features words that have the same vowel sound as *star* and words with the ending *-ly*. It also provides practice reading the high-frequency words *wish*, *much*, *these*, and *work*. After reading this book with your child, have him or her read aloud the words with the *-ly* ending.

Phonics Skills: *R*-controlled *ar*; Suffix *-ly*

High-Frequency Words: *wish, much, these, work*

Many people study the stars.
You can too.
Start now!
Look up at the sky tonight.

12

Stars

by Maggie Bridger
illustrated by Tom Barrett

Scott Foresman

Editorial Offices: Glenview, Illinois • New York, New York
Sales Offices: Reading, Massachusetts • Duluth, Georgia
Glenview, Illinois • Carrollton, Texas • Menlo Park, California

Look at this dark night sky.
You see lots and lots of stars!
Some people wish on these stars.
Some people study them.

You can make your own map.
Make a night sky.
Mark the stars you see.

Some stars have names.
You can read books about the stars.
Some books have charts.
Some have maps of the sky.

There is a lot to know about stars.
It's hard work.
But it's fun!

Go out at night.
Look up at the sky.
Watch the stars!

Stars seem to move slowly.
But they are really going quickly.

Stars seem to be very small.
But they really are very big.
Many are bigger than the sun.
Some are much bigger!
They are just far, far away.

This yard has too much light.
You can hardly see the stars.
The stars shine dimly.

Go where there are not many lights.
Try a park.
You will see the stars much better.

Start looking at stars nightly.
Watch them weekly.
Star watching is so much fun!

Scott Foresman
Reading

Grade 1
Phonics Reader 32

Fox and Stork
retold by
Myka-Lynne Sokoloff
illustrated by
Marvin Glass

Phonics Skills:
• *R*-controlled *or;* Inflected
  endings *-s, -es, -ed, -ing*
  (with and without
  spelling changes: drop *e*
  before *-ed, -ing*)

Scott Foresman
Phonics
System

Scott Foresman

Fox and Stork

retold by Myka-Lynne Sokoloff
illustrated by Marvin Glass

This book belongs to

_____

Phonics for Families: This book features words with the vowel sound heard in *stork* and *north*; words with the endings *-s, -es, -ed, -ing*, as in *liked, teaches, asked,* and *eating;* and the high-frequency words *would, cold, full, off,* and *before*. Read the story aloud with your child. Then ask your child to find all the words that have the same vowel sound as *stork.* You might also like to talk about the lesson being taught in this story.

Phonics Skills: *R*-controlled *or;* Inflected endings *-s, -es, -ed, -ing* (with and without spelling changes: drop *e* before *-ed, -ing*)

High-Frequency Words: *would, cold, full, off, before*

"I hope this teaches you, Fox. Treat me as you would like to be treated."

Fox and Stork

retold by Myka-Lynne Sokoloff
illustrated by Marvin Glass

Scott Foresman

Editorial Offices: Glenview, Illinois • New York, New York
Sales Offices: Reading, Massachusetts • Duluth, Georgia
Glenview, Illinois • Carrollton, Texas • Menlo Park, California

Fox was leaving the shop.

Would you like to eat with me?

Will we eat in your home or mine?

Stork ate and ate from the jar.
Soon she was full.
Fox was no more full than before.

Off Fox went to Stork's home.

Fox started to eat.

The meal was too cold.

The jar was too tall.

His nose did not fit.

Fox did not eat at all!

"Mine," said Fox.

Stork nodded.

"Hot or cold?" asked Fox.
Stork liked cold meals.
"Cold is good," said Stork.
"Well, we will see," said Fox.

"Hot or cold?" asked Stork.
"Hot is good," said Fox.
"Well, we will see," said Stork.

The next day, Stork saw Fox.

Would you come for a meal?

I would be happy to come.

Fox lived up north.
It was very cold up there.
He made what he liked to eat.
He made a hot dish of pork.

Stork started eating.
The meal was too hot.
The plate was too flat.
Her beak would not fit!
Stork stopped eating.
She did not eat a bit!

"I'm full," said Fox.
Stork was not full.
Stork was not happy.

Scott Foresman
Reading

Grade 1
Phonics Reader 33

**Cowgirl Gert and the
Dust Storm**
by Deborah Eaton
illustrated by
Drew-Brook-Cormack

Phonics Skills:
• *R*-controlled *-er, -ir, -ur*
• Comparative endings *-er*
and *-est*

Scott Foresman
**Phonics
System**

Scott Foresman

Cowgirl Gert and
the Dust Storm

by Deborah Eaton
illustrated by Drew-Brook-Cormack

This book belongs to

_____

Phonics for Families: This book provides practice in reading words with *er, ir,* and *ur,* as in *her, girl,* and *turn;* words with the comparative endings *er* and *est,* as in *darker* and *fastest;* and the high-frequency words *each, other, once, under,* and *which.* Have fun reading the story with your child. Then ask your child to make a list of all the words with *er, ir,* and *ur.*

Phonics Skills: *R*-controlled *-er, -ir, -ur;* Comparative endings *-er* and *-est*

High-Frequency Words: *each, other, once, under, which*

Yes, sir!
That Gert was some cowgirl!

Cowgirl Gert and the Dust Storm

by Deborah Eaton

illustrated by Drew-Brook-Cormack

Scott Foresman

Editorial Offices: Glenview, Illinois • New York, New York
Sales Offices: Reading, Massachusetts • Duluth, Georgia
Glenview, Illinois • Carrollton, Texas • Menlo Park, California

Gert was a cowgirl.
And let me tell you.
Gert was the best in the West!

Gert rode that storm.
And she sent it on its way.
Thanks to Gert, no one was hurt.
But first she made it dig a hole.
And we all got a brand new well!

Up, up, up she flew.
The storm twisted.
It turned under her.
But Gert held on.
"Yippee!" she yelled.
She was having fun!

Once Gert needed a brighter light.
So she just roped the moon!

That girl was sweeter than candy.
Once she met up with a bobcat.
My, my! He was a mean one!
They looked at each other.
Gert smiled.
And that old cat started to purr!

Quick as a wink, there she was.
Gert walked under that storm.
She had a saddle in her hands.

Dirt flew.

Trees hugged each other.

The corn turned inside out.

Thirty crows blew away.

A herd of goats flew off.

Which way would the storm go next?

"Gert!" I yelled.

Gert rode anything.

Yes, sir!

She rode the fastest horse.

She rode the meanest bull.

Once she even rode a dust storm.

It was hotter than hot.

We had not seen a drop of rain.

Then one day, a big storm blew in.

It was darker than night.

That storm started to turn.

It started to whirl and swirl.

Faster and faster it went!

Scott Foresman
Reading

Grade 1
Phonics Reader 34

Funny Clowns
by Anastasia Suen
illustrated by
John Manders

Phonics Skills:
• Vowel diphthong *ow/ou/*
• Medial consonants
  (two-syllable words)

Scott Foresman
Phonics System

Scott Foresman

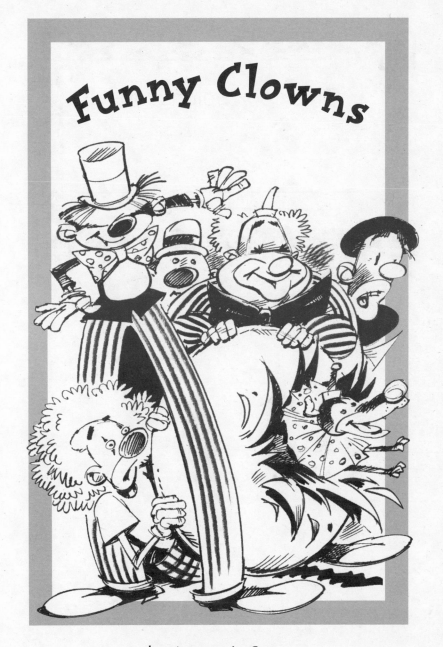

Funny Clowns

by Anastasia Suen
illustrated by John Manders

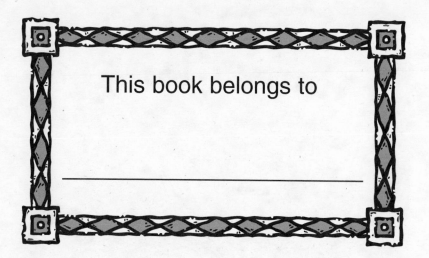

This book belongs to

_____

Phonics for Families: This book provides practice reading words with the vowel sound heard in *clown* and spelled with the letters *ow*; words with two syllables; and the high-frequency words *pull, goes, great, idea,* and *along*. Read the book together. Then have your child name words that rhyme with *clown*.

Phonics Skill: Vowel diphthong *ow/ou/*; Medial consonants (two-syllable words)

High-Frequency Words: *pull, goes, great, idea, along*

13

All the clowns take a bow.

It is time to go.

They had a great time.

They hope you did too.

Funny Clowns

by Anastasia Suen
illustrated by John Manders

Scott Foresman

Editorial Offices: Glenview, Illinois • New York, New York
Sales Offices: Reading, Massachusetts • Duluth, Georgia
Glenview, Illinois • Carrollton, Texas • Menlo Park, California

Do you like clowns?
They make work look like fun.
How do they do that?
Come along and see!

Look at these clowns.
They all ride together.
Ten clowns in one little car!
Now that's a crowd!

This clown likes to go fishing.
He puts his line down in the water.
Soon he feels a tug.
He pulls out a shark!
He'd better run for his life!

Clowns paint their faces.
They put on silly wigs.
They look in their trunks.
What do they find?
Lots and lots of funny things!

Clowns act silly for the crowd.

They make the crowd laugh.

The workmen pull things around.

The crowd doesn't watch them.

They watch the clowns.

The clowns are so funny!

These two clowns have a race.

It looks as if one ran out of gas!

The other one wins the race.

This clown can't find the rabbit.
He looks under his brown cape.
He turns the hat upside down.
Where is the rabbit?
It is eating a carrot!

8

Clowns like to play tricks.
This clown has a little can.
He pulls on the top.
Out pop some fake snakes!

Look at this clown with a crown.
Don't try this at home.
It's not a good idea!
This is no way to ride a bike!

6

What are the clowns doing now?
There is a fire!
"Jump," yell the firemen.
"Here she comes," they cry.
"There she goes!" they yell.

7

Scott Foresman
Reading

Grade 1
Phonics Reader 35

**How Hound
Became Happy**
by Patricia A. Keeler
illustrated by
Eldon Doty

Phonics Skills:
- Vowel diphthong *ou*/ou/
- Medial consonants
  (two-syllable words)

Scott Foresman
**Phonics
System**

Scott Foresman

How Hound
Became Happy

by Patricia A. Keeler
illustrated by Eldon Doty

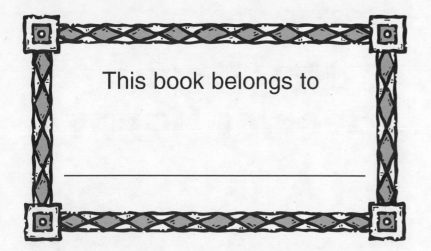

This book belongs to

_____

Phonics for Families: This book features words that have the vowel sound heard in the beginning of *out* and two-syllable words, such as *paper* and *became*. It also provides practice reading the high-frequency words *knew*, *picture*, *thought*, and *took*. Read the book together. Then ask your child to find words in the book that rhyme with *house*.

Phonics Skills: Vowel diphthong *ou* /ou/; Medial consonants (focus on decoding two-syllable words)

High-Frequency Words: *knew, picture, thought, took*

Hound ran and ran. He
played around in the grass.
Then he curled up to rest. He
was the picture of a happy dog!

12

How Hound Became Happy

by Patricia A. Keeler
illustrated by Eldon Doty

Scott Foresman

Editorial Offices: Glenview, Illinois • New York, New York
Sales Offices: Reading, Massachusetts • Duluth, Georgia
Glenview, Illinois • Carrollton, Texas • Menlo Park, California

Hound wasn't happy. He had to do something. So Hound thought and thought.

Then Hound had an idea!
He took out brushes and paper.
He painted a picture of grass.
Then he jumped into the picture.

The spotted dog barked too much.
The little dogs cried. They cried
louder and louder. "Ouch!"
shouted Hound. "You are hurting
my ears."

He had an idea! Hound took
out brushes and paper. He painted a
picture of money. Then he reached
into the picture.

Hound took out all the money.
He counted it.
Hound shouted, "I'm rich!"

4

One dog was a grouch. He liked
to sleep on the couch. He liked to
sleep in the sun. He pouted when
the clouds hid the sun.

9

Hound took the dogs home with him. Now he wasn't lonely. He had lots of friends. But Hound still wasn't happy!

Hound got a big house. But he still wasn't happy!

He looked around his big house. Hound was the only one there!

Hound had an idea! He knew what to do. Hound painted a new picture. It was a picture of a dog pound.

Hound jumped into the picture. He let all the dogs out!

Scott Foresman
Reading

Grade 1
Phonics Reader 36

Roy Goes Camping
by Betsy Franco
illustrated by
Amy Wummer

Phonics Skills:
• Vowel diphthongs *oi, oy*
• Multisyllabic words
(compounds, contractions,
inflected endings)

Scott Foresman
Phonics System

Scott Foresman

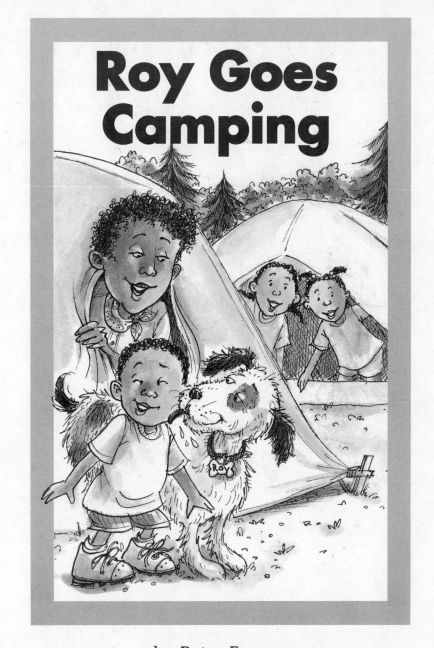

Roy Goes Camping

by Betsy Franco
illustrated by Amy Wummer

This book belongs to

_____

Phonics for Families: This book gives your child practice in reading words with the letters *oy* and *oi*, as in *boy* and *spoil*; words with more than one syllable, such as *campfire* and *isn't*; and the high-frequency words *boy*, *school*, *open*, *move*, and *always*. Have your child read the book with you. Then ask your child to find words that rhyme with *boy* (*Roy*, *Troy*, *Joy*) and *boil* (*foil*, *oil*, *spoil*, *soil*).

Phonics Skill: Vowel diphthongs *oi, oy;* Multisyllabic words (compounds, contractions); Inflected endings

High-Frequency Words: *boy*, *school*, *open*, *move*, *always*

Then it was time to go. Joy
pointed to a rainbow.
She shouted, "We had fun!
Not one thing spoiled our trip!"

Roy Goes Camping

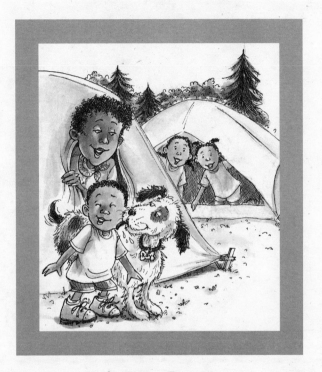

by Betsy Franco
illustrated by Amy Wummer

Scott Foresman

Editorial Offices: Glenview, Illinois • New York, New York
Sales Offices: Reading, Massachusetts • Duluth, Georgia
Glenview, Illinois • Carrollton, Texas • Menlo Park, California

"School starts in three days.
Let's go camping!" said Mom.
"Can Roy come?" asked Kim.
"Yes," said Mom.

"We don't have raincoats,"
said Mom. "But rain will not
spoil our trip!"

Kim said, "Roy enjoys the toast! He enjoys the eggs too! Good boy, Roy."

Everyone packed the car. Troy got his toys. Kim got the foil and oil. Joy got the sleeping bags.

It was getting late. They were lost. Joy found a map. She pointed to the campground.

© Scott Foresman 1

"The boiled eggs are fine. The toast is burned," said Joy. "But the toast isn't that bad. It will not spoil our trip!"

In the morning, they made
a fire. They boiled eggs. They
made toast on the foil.

"There's one spot left," said Kim.
"The spot isn't very big. But we'll
fit. It will not spoil our trip!"

They made a campfire. Roy
started digging in the soil.
Kim yelled, "Move, Roy,
move! You can't spoil our trip!"

6

Troy wouldn't sleep.
"Noise is fine," Mom said.
"There's always noise. Noise will
not spoil our trip!"

7